God Is Like...

Kenneth L. Gibble

CSS Publishing Company, Inc.
Lima, Ohio

GOD IS LIKE

FIRST EDITION
Copyright © 2023
by CSS Publishing Co., Inc.

The original purchaser may print and photocopy material in this publication for use as it was intended (worship material for worship use; educational material for classroom use; dramatic material for staging or production). No additional permission is required from the publisher for such copying by the original purchaser only. Inquiries should be addressed to: Permissions, CSS Publishing Company, Inc., 5450 N. Dixie Highway, Lima, Ohio 45807.

Library of Congress Cataloging-in-Publication Data

Names: Gibble, Kenneth L., 1941- author.
Title: God is like / Ken Gibble.
Description: First edition. | Lima, Ohio : CSS Publishing Company, Inc., [2023]
Identifiers: LCCN 2022054210 (print) | LCCN 2022054211 (ebook) | ISBN 9780788030741 | ISBN 9780788030758 (ebook)
Subjects: LCSH: God--Biblical teaching. | Metaphor in the Bible.
Classification: LCC BS544 .G53 2023 (print) | LCC BS544 (ebook) | DDC 231--dc23/eng/20230309
LC record available at https://lccn.loc.gov/2022054210
LC ebook record available at https://lccn.loc.gov/2022054211

For more information about CSS Publishing Company resources, visit our website at www.csspub.com, email us at csr@csspub.com, or call (800) 241-4056.

e-book:
ISBN-13: 978-0-7880-3075-8
ISBN-10: 0-7880-3075-2

ISBN-13: 978-0-7880-3074-1
ISBN-10: 0-7880-3074-4   PRINTED IN U.S.A.

Contents

GOD IS LIKE ... A NAME
Exodus 3:1-15 5

GOD IS LIKE ... A POTTER
Jeremiah 18:1-11; 1 Corinthians 15:20-26 11

GOD IS LIKE ... BREAD
Joel 2:23-30; John 6:25-35 17

GOD IS LIKE ... A PARENT
Hosea 11:1-4; Luke 15:1-32 21

GOD IS LIKE ... FIRE
Malachi 3:1-4; Luke 3:1-6,9,16-17 27

GOD IS LIKE ... A COMFORTER
2 Corinthians 1:3-7 33

GOD IS LIKE ... A FACE
Genesis 33:1-11; 2 Corinthians 4:5-6 39

GOD IS LIKE ... A FRIEND
2 Corinthians 5:16-20 45

GOD IS LIKE ... A LAMB
Exodus 12:3-8; Luke 22:7-20 51

GOD IS LIKE ...
Isaiah 40:18-31; John 1:1-14 57

GOD IS LIKE ... A NAME

Exodus 3:1-15

A while back, I came across a journal that had three words on the cover to announce its theme. The three words were "God is like," followed by an ellipsis ... three dots. Each page, with the help of a poem or a scripture passage or a prayer, completed that sentence. God is like... fire, God is like... a word, God is like... a friend, God is like... a shepherd, and so on. It was a great way to grasp, if only in a partial way, the divine mystery we call God.

And it gave me an idea for a sermon series. My purpose is simply to help all of us appreciate and understand more about God and to discover appropriate responses to this holy one. I hope our exploration will provide both comfort and challenge. And I think a word of warning is in order: we should be prepared for some surprises along the way, because the older I get, the more I keep discovering that both the universe we live in and the God who created and loves it are far more complex and far more wonderful than we usually think or can even imagine.

We begin our exploration today with some thoughts on the idea that God is like... a name. Not just any name, of course, but God's name. I realize this is a rather curious way to think about God, that God is like God's name. At first thought, it may seem like nonsense. So to get some clues to this notion, that God is like a name, we need to pay close attention to words in our Old Testament scripture text. It's a famous story, about Moses and the burning bush. As you listen, I want you to pay special attention to the conversation between Moses and the Lord, especially when Moses asked for the name of the one who was speaking to him.

It's a very old story, a story in which a divine being spoke directly to Moses. Notice that when the voice from the bush called Moses by name, we are told that Moses hid his face because he was afraid to look at God. Ancient belief had it that any mortal who looked on a god would be struck blind or would die.

The voice told Moses, "I am the God of Abraham, the God of Isaac, and the God of Jacob. I have observed the misery of my people who are in Egypt... I will send you to Pharaoh to bring my people, the Israelites, out of Egypt."

In other words, this deity was a tribal god, a god worshiped by the tribe of people who were descendants of a man named Abraham, a tribe of people known as the Israelites. The world in which they lived, in which Moses lived, was a world filled with the worship of many gods. People in that time believed that human life was surrounded and influenced by a variety of divine powers. But this wasn't necessarily comforting because some of those divine powers brought calamity and suffering. If you were dealing with a god, you had better know what kind of god it was. Furthermore, it was a good idea to know the deity's name so you could call upon it, and therefore have at least a measure of control over it.

This explains the question Moses directed to the voice speaking to him from the burning bush. Moses wanted to know the name of the god who was speaking to him. But Moses was clever. He didn't want to offend this deity by asking his questions directly. So he asked his question indirectly. "If I come to the Israelites," asked Moses, "and say to them, 'The God of your ancestors has sent me to you,' and they ask me, 'What is his name?' what shall I say to them?"

See what Moses was doing? He wanted to know the name of this strange deity that spoke from a bush that burned but was not consumed. By knowing the name, Moses would be able to call upon the deity and Moses would also get a clue to the nature of this god. In ancient time, the names of persons or gods revealed a great deal about them. Names carried with them information about character and personality. So Moses engaged in a battle of wits with this god. The voice of the deity had said it had chosen Moses to lead the Israelites out of Egypt. Needless to say, Moses was hardly thrilled at that prospect. The Pharaoh of Egypt was a powerful person, not someone to be trifled with. Remember that Moses himself had grown up in the palace of Pharaoh as an adopted child. Moses knew that anybody who took on the assignment this god was proposing could get into big, big trouble.

"Okay," Moses answered the voice, "you say I'm to lead the Israelites out of Egypt. When I go and tell them all this, the first thing they'll want to know is the name of the god that spoke to me. What will I tell them?"

And then came one of the holiest, most momentous pronouncements in the Bible. The voice said to Moses, "I AM WHO I AM. Thus you shall say to the Israelites, 'I AM has sent me to you.'" Moses wanted to know the name of the god and this was the answer Moses received. The name of the god was I AM WHO I AM.

We need to take a close look at this name. The Hebrew language contains no vowels, only consonants. The Hebrew letters that form the name of the deity here are YHWH. We pronounce it Yahweh. What those letters mean in Hebrew is "I am who I am" or "I will be what I will be."

What a strange and wonderful name. The name announced that this God was free from human control. I AM WHO I AM meant that God was God. God was and *is* not mortal. God cannot fully be known by human beings. Furthermore, God is present, not absent. I AM. This name was entrusted to Moses and to God's people. They alone knew the divine name and could call upon it.

In fact, down through the centuries and up to the present time, the people of Israel, the people known in our day as Jews, have regarded this name as so holy that they do not pronounce it, even in their worship. Instead of saying "Yahweh," they say "Adonai," a name which most English translations give as "Lord."

This passage we have been studying from Exodus told us something about God. It told us that the name of God was important; it was holy. The name established the identity of God. But what did all this have to do with my life and your life? What difference does it make to know something about God's name?

One way it matters has to do with something way back in the second chapter of Genesis. There we learn that human beings were created in the image of God. That meant if God had a name and an identity, so do you, so do I! And this name, this identity, was and is extremely important.

I AM WHO I AM. That is God's name. And, in a smaller way — a much smaller, but still important way — that is your name and my name too. We are who we are. Unique. Unrepeatable. There is no one just like you before or since. It's worth getting paying attention to.

The great Christian mystic of the Middle Ages, Meister Eckhart, wrote:

That I am a man
I have in common with all men,
That I see and hear
and eat and drink
I share with all animals.
But that I am I is exclusively mine,
And belongs to me
And to nobody else,
To no other man
Nor to an angel nor to God,
Except inasmuch as I am one with him. (in the public domain)

You and I are created in the image of God, with a unique identity. Discovering that identity, learning exactly who we are is a lifelong process. The teenage years are especially devoted to discovery of identity, but the process really does go on all through our lives. And discovery is the right word for it. It's almost like that parable Jesus told about the man who found a treasure hidden in a field or a pearl of great price. The discovery was a cause for great rejoicing. Learning who you are, discovering the unique gifts God has given you and being grateful for this discovery, are important elements of faith.

Just as each of us has an identity, we also have names. Names are important. Doesn't it feel good to hear your name spoken by a friend? Doesn't it irritate you when the phone rings and somebody you've never met, somebody trying to sell you something, uses your first name? You are offended and rightly so because your name is part of you; it should be used with care.

Parents usually give lots of thought to the names they give their children. Were you named after someone — a relative, a famous person, or a character in the Bible? Most names parents give their children say something important about the hopes those parents have for their offspring or about the values they hope they children will have when they grow up.

Names should never be taken lightly. You call a person what that person wants to be called. If he prefers James, don't call him Jim. When you are introduced to a person for the first time, pronounce the name carefully. This is especially important when you meet someone who speaks another language. If a man tells you his name is Francisco, don't call him Frankie unless he tells you he prefers that nickname.

Years ago when I began attending seminary, one of the seniors took to calling me Kenny. That had been my name when I was a youngster. As an adult I preferred "Ken." His calling me "Kenny" irritated me because it seemed to be his way of reminding me I was a mere beginning student. Afterward we'd see each other about once a year at a church conference. I'd grit my teeth when I saw him coming because I knew he'd say, "Well, Kenny, how's it going?" Only in recent years has he finally stopped using that name.

Jesus had a name, of course. "Jesus" is the Greek form of the name Joshua, a Hebrew name which means "the one who will save." I remember one of the preachers in my home church doing a whole sermon in which he did nothing more than list all the names believers have given to Jesus: Savior, Master, Lily of the Valley, Prince of Peace, Bright and Morning Star. Very little commentary was in his sermon, just a list of names for Jesus. It went on and on and finally got kind of boring, but it illustrated how much Christians have loved Jesus and how many names they have known him by.

The name of Jesus is precious to Christians. But everything in creation has a name. Psalm 147 includes this lovely verse: "The Lord telleth the number of the stars; he calleth them all by their names" (v. 4 KJV). I love that imagery of the Creator counting the millions, billions of stars in space and calling each one by name.

I am who I am, that is my name, said God. The book of Revelation picked up this theme. "I am the first and the last," said the Lord God Almighty, "who is, who was, and who is to come" (Revelation 1:8 TEV). Or, as my mother told me when I was a child, "God always was and God always will be." In Revelation there is another image, that of the faithful having their names written in the Lamb's book of life (Revelation 21:27). Don't you love that thought? Our *names* are *written* there. No long numerical codes, no social security numbers. Our names are there, spelled correctly and pronounced lovingly by the one whose name is I AM, the one who knows the name of every far-flung star.

God is like... a name. Not just any name, but the holy name. This God loves us and knows us by name. Thanks be to God. May God's holy name be praised.

GOD IS LIKE ... A POTTER

Jeremiah 18:1-11; 1 Corinthians 15:20-26

The word that came to Jeremiah from the Lord: "Come, go down to the potter's house, and there I will let you hear my words."

So begins our morning's reading from the Old Testament. When you hear those words, you may wonder what the Bible meant when it said, "The word that came to Jeremiah from the Lord." How did that word come to Jeremiah? Was it written down somewhere? Did Jeremiah hear it audibly? Just who was this Jeremiah anyway and why did the word of the Lord come to him?

Lots of questions come to mind. They are questions that deserve some attention before we go any further. Let's start with the last question about Jeremiah's identity. Jeremiah was a prophet who lived in the kingdom of Judah about six centuries before Christ. He was the son of a priest, but when still a young man, the Bible says, Yahweh called him to be a prophet. The nature of that call is recorded in the opening verses of the book that bears Jeremiah's name.

> Now the word of the Lord came to me saying, "Before I formed you in the womb I knew you, and before you were born I consecrated you; I appointed you a prophet to the nations."
>
> Then I said, "Ah, Lord God! Truly I do not know how to speak, for I am only a boy."
>
> But the Lord said to me, "Do not say, 'I am only a boy'; for you shall go to all to whom I send you, and you shall speak whatever I command you, Do not be afraid of them, for I am
> with you to deliver you, says the Lord."

Then the Lord put out his hand and touched my mouth; and the Lord said to me, "Now I have put my words in your mouth. See, today I appoint you over nations and over kingdoms, to pluck up and to pull down, to destroy and to overthrow, to build and to plant." (Jeremiah 1:410)

In these words, Jeremiah told us several things about his vocation as a prophet. First, it was not something he chose. God chose him. Secondly, Jeremiah did not want to become a prophet; he tried to beg off as being too young. Thirdly, God refused to listen to Jeremiah's protests; instead, God promised to be with him. Finally, God reached out and touched Jeremiah's mouth and told him God's words would be in his mouth, words that would have power to create and to destroy.

How did such a wondrous and fearful message come to Jeremiah? Judging from the content of Jeremiah's words, it was probably a vivid dream or a vision. In ancient times, dreams and visions were regarded as a means for a deity to communicate with mortals.

As we read through the book of Jeremiah we soon discover that the vocation of prophet did not give him much happiness. The message Jeremiah was given to speak consisted mostly of gloom and doom. The nation will suffer punishment for its wrongdoing, Jeremiah kept saying.

As you can guess, that message did not win him many friends in high places. Before his career ended, Jeremiah would endure the hostility of most of his countrymen, he would spend time in prison and would die in exile. The time he lived in was a difficult one for prophets who spoke the word of the Lord. And yet, after his death, the people of Israel realized that his message was so important, so truthful, so clearly inspired by God, that his words came to be honored as a valuable part of holy scripture for the Hebrew people and, later, for Christians.

One of the best-known of Jeremiah's writings was his account of what happened when the Lord told him to visit the potter's house. Jeremiah reported what he saw there.

So I went down to the potter's house, and there he was working at his wheel. The vessel he was
making of clay was spoiled in the potter's hand, and he reworked it into another vessel, as
seemed good to him (Jeremiah 18:4).

It was while he was watching the potter at work that the word of the Lord came again to Jeremiah. The Lord said:

Can I not do with you, O house of Israel, just as this potter has done? Just like the clay in the
potter's hand, so are you in my hand, O house of Israel. (Jeremiah 18:56)

In this well-known verse, God is a potter, the one who molds nations and the people in them just as a potter molds the clay on the potter's wheel.

What is God like? That's a question we have been considering. Today we turn our attention to the idea of God as a potter.

One thing we must recognize is that no image of God will be adequate in and of itself to encompass all that God is. In fact, that's why the biblical writers kept reaching for new words to represent the God they worshiped: fire, cloud, eagle, father, mother, thunder, shepherd, king. None of those words, those images, was sufficient. Other words and symbols came into play. I use that word "play" deliberately. Because it *is* something like a holy game, this trying to find words to speak of God. It's almost like a game of hide and seek, with the holy one always eluding our grasp, slipping away just when we think we've captured the essence of the divine with a word, a phrase, a symbol.

Let us play this game with the elusive one: God as a potter.

If you've ever watched a potter at work, you've probably marveled that he or she was able to make something out of nothing. Not really nothing, but a lump of clay seems almost nothing. The potter threw the clay onto the wheel and then set the wheel turning. Very soon, the potter's skilled hands transformed that lump into a something. You're not sure what: will it be a jug, a bowl, a cup, or a pitcher?

Then, when the potter was finished, you felt like applauding. Here was a new creation; a vase, let's say. That blob of wet clay had been transformed into something lovely and useful. Incredible!

God is a potter. God makes something out of nothing. In the book of Genesis, we read that God formed Adam, which means "man," a human being, from the dust of the earth. God is portrayed there as a divine potter at work on earthly clay. Whereas the rest of creation comes into being by the speaking of God's word, to create the human creature, God scooped clay from the riverbank, touched and molded it and then breathed into it the breath of life. God was intimately involved with our creation, the ancient tale told us.

Job attested to this understanding of God. In one of his prayers, Job said to God: "Remember that you fashioned me like clay" (Job 10:9a). Isaiah echoes the same thought with his words: "Yet, O Lord, you are our Father; we are the clay, and you are our potter; we are all the work of your hand" (Isaiah 64:8).

When we read Jeremiah's account of what he saw in the potter's house and the word he received there from the Lord, we quickly grasp the idea of God the potter as creator, the one who makes all things.

What we tend to overlook, because it isn't nearly so pleasant, is another aspect of God the potter. God is not only a creator; God is also a destroyer.

In many ancient religions, the powers beyond human understanding were distributed among many gods. One god sent rain, another blessed a family with children, yet another was prayed to for healing. There were also gods that brought calamity. There was a god of flood, of famine, and of war. The Hebrews worshiped one god, Yahweh. This God encompassed all power, both the power of creation and the power of destruction.

These days we get a little uncomfortable talking about God as destroyer. For many of us, it brings back childhood ideas of God as judge, as punisher. This was a God not to be loved as much as it was a God to be feared.

But read the verses in Jeremiah carefully. You'll see that the prophet was mostly concerned about showing the holy potter's ability to destroy. Rarely does a potter at the wheel create a vessel to his or her satisfaction on the first try. Frequently the potter will squash a piece of half-formed clay and begin all over again.

At the end of Jeremiah's account of what God revealed to him at the potter's house, we find these words:

> Thus says the Lord: Look, I am a potter shaping evil against you and devising a plan against you. Turn now, all of you from your evil way, and amend your ways and your doings.

We discover that the whole point of Jeremiah's trip to the potter's house was a warning for the people of Judah. Jeremiah was reminding them that the Lord had power to crush them as a potter crushes the clay on the potter's wheel.

God as destroyer — not a welcome thought to many people. And yet the power to destroy is an undeniable attribute of God. Without it, God is reduced to a good-natured uncle, an indulgent aunt. Someone who tells us: hey, you're okay; you deserve a break today; don't worry, be happy.

Sometimes you and I need to hear messages like that. Sometimes, but not all the time. There are also times when you and I need to hear a warning. We need to be told that what we are thinking or doing or failing to do can destroy us. If your health habits are killing you, you don't want a doctor who says, "Eat and drink anything you like." You want the doctor to give it to you straight, and you want advice on how to improve your health. If your performance at work is going downhill, you don't want a supervisor who just lets you self-destruct. You want a warning, and you want help on getting back on track.

If self-centeredness, laziness, or cynicism have weakened your spiritual health, you don't want a preacher or a church or a God that says, "Hey, your faith is your own business; it doesn't really matter what you believe or what you do."

The words of a hymn by Isaac Watts present a striking alternative:

> Before Jehovah's awe-full throne,
> Ye nations bow with sacred joy;
> Know that the Lord is God alone;
> He can create and He destroy,
> He can create and He destroy. (in the public domain)

What does God destroy? Evil in its great variety of forms. "Deliver us from evil," we pray. And what we mean is there are those things in the world and in our own lives that threaten us, conspire against us. Deliver us, O Lord, from these things. Paul writes in 1 Corinthians that, in the end, God will destroy all the things that have plagued humanity. And the last enemy to be destroyed is death.

Have you ever prayed for God to destroy something? I don't mean to destroy another person. I mean to destroy something in your life. Because you are human, you have things in your life that ought to die. Maybe it's an irrational fear. Maybe it's a violent temper. Maybe it's a poor self-image. Maybe it's a crippling addiction. Maybe it's your compulsion to be a perfectionist.

Let's spend a few moments in silence now. I'm going to start a prayer, and then I invite each of you to finish the prayer with your own silent ending. Let us pray.

> O God, Holy Potter, you create and you destroy. I thank you for creating me. I thank you for your power to destroy in me that which needs to die. Hear my prayer now and destroy in me.

[Silent Prayers]

Amen.

GOD IS LIKE ... BREAD

Joel 2:23-30; John 6:25-35

How does one speak of God? Humankind has been trying to do that ever since it first discovered language. To speak of God is to attempt the impossible. Human language is inadequate to express what our minds and spirits can only dimly comprehend.

But still we must try to speak of God. We must. Otherwise, we can never be fully human, all that we are meant to be.

We try to speak of God, the divine mystery. And because God is mystery, we should not be surprised if our attempts to speak of this mystery often sound childlike. People of ancient times saw that the sun and rain made plants grow and so they worshipped the sun and the rain as gods. Other ancient peoples wondered how the world and sky came to be and so they worshipped a god they called the Maker, the Creator. They knew they could not live without food to eat, without bread. And so they worshipped a god they called the giver of food, of bread.

An ancient people known as the Hebrews believed their God intervened directly into human affairs. When their God (they called their god Yahweh), saw them doing evil, they believed he punished them. When they did good, he rewarded them. One of the Hebrew prophets, whose name was Joel, saw the hand of Yahweh in an onslaught of locusts. Listen to his description of what the locusts did to the land.

> What the cutting locust left,
> the swarming locust has eaten.
>
> What the swarming locust left,
> the hopping locust has eaten,
> and what the hopping locust left,
> the destroying locust has eaten.

> Wake up, you drunkards, and weep;
> and wail, all you wine-drinkers,
> over the sweet wine,
> for it is cut off from your mouth.
>
> For a nation has invaded my land, powerful and
> innumerable;
> its teeth are lions' teeth,
> and it has the fangs of a lioness.
>
> It has laid waste my vines,
> and splintered my fig trees;
> it has stripped off their bark and thrown it down;
> their branches have turned white. (Joel 1:4-7)

Yes, devastation has come to the land, but all is not lost, said the prophet Joel. If the nation will leave its wicked ways and seek Yahweh's favor, if the people will return to the Lord in repentance, who knows whether the Lord will not turn and relent and give a blessing?

Then the prophet speaks on behalf of the Lord. It is a message of assurance and promise we heard in our Old Testament lesson of the morning.

> You shall eat in plenty and be satisfied, and praise the
> name of the Lord your God (Joel 1:2-6a).

The people called Hebrews believed their god was the giver of every good gift and of life itself. The air they breathed, the food they ate — all of it came from the hand of the Lord. One of their poets put it this way:

> [Lord,] You cause the grass to grow for the cattle,
> and plants for people to use,
> to bring forth food from the earth,
> and wine to gladden the human heart,
> oil to make the face shine,
> and bread to strengthen the human heart
> (Psalm 104:14-15).

It really isn't surprising that the Hebrew people believed their god was the giver of the bread they ate. We human creatures cannot survive without food. And yet my guess is that some skeptics way back in ancient times scoffed at the idea that food came from God.

Wait a minute, they probably said. I earned this bread by the sweat of my own brow. God didn't give me this food, I got it for myself. And then some wise old man or woman said to the doubter, "Yes, but who gave you the strength to earn your bread? Who gave you hands to earn it with? Are you foolish enough to think you gave yourself life?"

God is the giver of bread. We still believe it. Our prayers express it. "Give us this day our daily bread," we pray. And our prayer is a way of saying what we believe …that human life and the resources to sustain it are gifts from the hand of God.

But the title of this sermon goes a step further. It states that God is like …bread. Not just that God is the giver of bread, but that God is like bread. Whatever can that mean?

I said at the beginning that God is mystery. And what a mystery it was when the man from Nazareth came to town and performed many signs. According to John's gospel, Jesus once fed a crowd of people, using only five loaves and two fish. That got everyone talking. They came to Jesus and told him they thought he was something special all right and they'd like to see what other spectacular things he could do. Maybe if they stuck around, he'd feed them on a regular basis.

No, you're missing the point, Jesus said. "Do not work for the food that perishes, but for the food that endures to eternal life." That got them scratching their heads, all right.

Then he said: "My Father gives you the true bread from heaven, …[bread that] gives life to the world.

And they answered, "Sir, give us this bread always."

See, they still didn't get it. They were still thinking about their stomachs. So he said it as plainly as he could.

> I am the bread of life. Whoever comes to me will never be hungry, and whoever believes in me will never be thirsty (John 6:35).

When they heard those words, the light finally began to dawn. He wasn't talking about the bread that came out of the oven. This was another kind of bread, the kind that feeds the human heart.

Christ is the bread of heaven, we say. And what we mean is that he is the answer to the hunger of our hearts. You and I hunger for so many things — for inner peace, for meaning, for faith, for love. The hunger lies so deep in us we often can't even give it a name. We feel it mostly as a longing, a yearning for something we once had but have no longer have, or maybe we never had it. Many times we're hardly aware of the hunger, but at other times it is so intense, so sharp, that we feel it as physical pain.

What does Jesus mean when he says he is the bread of life and that whoever comes to him will never be hungry? I must confess to you that I don't know what he means.

But I believe when he says it, he is speaking to the deep spiritual hunger in all of us.

I believe that he was talking about the mystery of himself and of God.

I believe that the inner hunger we feel was put there by God so that we would seek and know and love God.

I believe that Augustine was right when he prayed:

> "Thou hast made us for thyself, and our hearts are restless until they find their rest in thee."
> I believe that we are right to call Jesus the bread of heaven.
> I believe that when we come to the Lord's table, it is our inner hunger that brings us here.
> And I believe God is like the bread that satisfies the deepest hunger of our hearts.

I invite you, I urge you, to bring your hunger, your thirst. Know it is Christ who bids you come. And I hope you will believe that God, in Christ, will not send you away empty.

GOD IS LIKE ... A PARENT

Hosea 11:1-4; Luke 15:1-32

What is God like? We've been exploring that question, each time with a different image for an answer. So far, we've thought about how God is like the words "I Am," how God is like a potter and how God is like bread.

Today we turn to an image that is probably more familiar than any other for most Christians — God as parent.

The religion of the Hebrews was not the first to regard God as father. Do you remember your Greek mythology, where Zeus was the father of the gods? And though we have no written records, historians tell us that the religion of many primitive peoples included worship of the Great Mother, from whose womb all things were born.

It was natural for people in early civilizations to think of the deity as a parent. For all children, there is a sense in which their parents are godlike. As a small child, I am very aware that my parents are older, bigger, wiser and more powerful than I am. So it's not surprising that the adherents of nearly every religion have attributed father and mother qualities to the gods they worship.

What is surprising, when we turn to the Old Testament, is how few are the references to God as father or mother. Hebrew culture was strongly patriarchal; men ran the show. Therefore, we would expect the Hebrew people to regard Yahweh as a male deity. And yet it isn't often that Yahweh was described as a father.

In our Old Testament reading from Hosea, the prophet is speaking on behalf of Yahweh. Listen again to some of the phrases.

> When Israel was a child, I loved him, and out of Egypt I called my son.... It was I who taught Ephraim to walk, I took them up in my arms.... I was to them like those who

lift infants to their cheeks. I bent down to them and fed them (from Hosea 11:1-4).

Here God speaks as a loving parent. Notice that God could be either a mother or a father in this passage. There is no way to tell which. But the point I want to make is that this is an untypical passage in the Old Testament. True, the book of Jeremiah has a verse in which God himself father of the nation of Israel (Jeremiah 31:9). And Isaiah contains a few scattered verses like this one in which the people address God:

You, O Lord, are our father; our Redeemer from of old is your name (Isaiah 63:16b).

And there's a lovely verse, also in Isaiah, where God says to the people of Israel:

As a mother comforts her child, so I will comfort you;
you shall be comforted in Jerusalem (Isaiah 66:13).

But that's about it. The Old Testament views God not as father of the natural world, not as father to all humanity, not as a heavenly parent who listens to the prayers of each individual. Rather, the Hebrews thought of God as father, and to a lesser extent, mother of their nation. As the father of his people Israel, Yahweh promised to protect them and care for them. Yahweh as divine parent was compassionate and loving, not cruel or unfeeling. The parent images of God in the Old Testament are positive images.

But when we come to the New Testament, we find a remarkable change. We are shown God as a father still caring and loving, but now the Heavenly Father is passionately concerned about everyone, not just the nation of Israel. The one responsible for this dramatic shift is Jesus.

Time after time, Jesus refers to God as a heavenly father. What kind of father is this God? Jesus says that the heavenly Father feeds the birds and clothes the fields with grass and will care for his human children in the same way.

Don't use lots of fancy words in your prayers, says Jesus, "for your Father knows what you need before you ask him" (Matthew. 6:8).

And Jesus said: "Are not two sparrows sold for a penny? Yet not one of them will fall to the ground apart from your Father. And even the hairs of your head are all counted. So do not be afraid; you are of more value than many sparrows" (Matthew 10:29-31).

The Heavenly Father cares not only for those who do good, those who worship and serve him. God as father loves all his children, even wayward children. Jesus said it like this:

"I say to you, Love your enemies and pray for those who persecute you, so that you may be children of your Father in heaven; for he makes his sun rise on the evil and on the good, and sends rain on the righteous and on the unrighteous" (Matthew. 5:44-45).

What kind of heavenly father is God? Perhaps the best answer Jesus gave to this question came in the parable we call the prodigal son. It is one of the most touching, beautiful stories in all of world literature. We're so familiar with it that we can miss the surprising behavior of the father.

He didn't scold the boy for leaving home and wasting his inheritance. He didn't say he hoped his son would never do something like that again. No, he ordered that something be brought for the wayward one to eat. He dismissed the boy's attempt to apologize by telling his servants to bring his son some proper clothes. All he could say was my boy was lost and now is found, he was dead but now he's alive.

Who is the father in the story? The gospel doesn't spell it out, but it was clear that Jesus was comparing the parable's merciful father to God, a merciful parent. It's the God of grace who doesn't demand an explanation for his wayward children.

The Father-God Jesus told about was not a god who demanded reparations, or who found it necessary to inflict punishment. This was God the loving Father who heals, who forgives, who nurtures. This was a God, who, in another parable, was depicted as a woman searching for a lost coin, as a shepherd seeking the lost sheep. This heavenly father loved the prodigal as much as he loved the son who stayed at home.

Jesus dared to use a term unheard of in his prayers to the Heavenly Father. He addressed God as "Abba." It's an intimate form of address. In English it can be translated "daddy." It's like a little plaque I saw in a gift shop when we were on vacation one summer. It said: "Anyone can be a father; it takes a special person to be a daddy." Jesus seemed to say we should address the heavenly parent the way children address their earthly parents: "Mommy and Daddy." That is, we should give God the respect due our parents — be ready to obey, but do so knowing we are supremely loved and cared for.

All this is just great, you may thinking, except for one little problem …what if my earthly parents weren't loving and caring? What if my father or mother or both were mostly cold and aloof, or too demanding, or irresponsible? What if my parents abandoned me? Even worse, what if they abused me emotionally, physically, or sexually? What then? What good will thinking of God as a divine parent be to be?

Such questions point up the inadequacy of the image of God as parent. We've discovered the same thing about each of the images of God we've considered so far. They all have pluses and minuses. The big minus in the idea of God as a parent is that no human parent is unconditionally good and loving or even consistent and fair. All human parents are just that …human. They make mistakes, some of them big mistakes. They sin against their children. They sometimes expected too much of their kids, they sometimes let them down.

I loved my parents. They gave me more to be thankful for than I could ever repay. But they damaged me too. It was inevitable, just as it is inevitable that in some ways all of us who are parents damage our own children.

And so while you and I can find comfort and assurance in thinking of God as our heavenly father or mother, we also must be aware of the limitations of this image. Your experience and your relationship with your parents colors your understanding of God. To the extent that you are angry at your parents or still rebelling against them or controlled by your experience with them, to that extent thinking of God as heavenly parent is not especially helpful.

Your spiritual health may require other images. There is a sense in which God as parent can hold us back. Yes, it may be comforting to think of God as the kind of heavenly father Jesus described. Each of us has a deep longing to return to the security of childhood when we were cradled, fed at our mother's breast, fussed over, when we were the center of our parents' attention. Our trust in a loving parent God is an expression of that longing, and that is fine.

But if that is all there is to our understanding of God, or if our religious understanding is mostly that, we will be stuck in spiritual childhood or spiritual adolescence. Parents, after all, do limit our freedom. It's part of their job. If you understand God mostly heavenly parent, you may not discover the freedom you were created to find. You may play it spiritually safe, trading the risks of newness and freedom for the comfort and security of what is known and understood.

Individuals can make this mistake, and so can churches. The church that lives by the motto, "We've always done it this way," has not moved beyond the image of God as parent. The person who refuses to consider new images of God will remain in spiritual childhood.

God is like a parent. Yes. We can still affirm that, still sing hymns like "Take My Hand and Lead Me, Father." We may even stretch ourselves with prayers and hymns that remind us of the mothering aspect of God. But let us be open to other images of the God who calls us to grow beyond God as parent, to stretch our minds and our faith.

> To use a phrase found in scripture, let us as individuals and a church "grow in the knowledge of God." (Colossians 1:10)

Yes, God is like a father, and that can be comforting. But God is also much more than even the best of fathers.

GOD IS LIKE ... FIRE

Malachi 3:1-4; Luke 3:1-6,9,16-17

When fire destroyed Grandpa Ober's barn, I was only three or four years old. I wasn't there to see the blaze, I'm not even sure the picture I have in my memory of charred logs is something I actually saw or merely the product of my imagination.

I do, however, remember hearing the story of what happened. My grandfather had one of those long white beards that many men his age wore back then. In fact when I heard the stories in Sunday school of Noah, Abraham, and Isaac and all those patriarchs in the Old Testament, I always imagined them looking something like Grandpa Ober. He was a farmer, and evidently a bit of a speculator, because from my earliest recollection, he owned a small handful of farms near Elizabethtown, Pennsylvania.

One afternoon he was working alone in the barn at the home farm. Apparently a spark from the tractor caught in a pile of straw and began to smolder. Grandpa tore off his coat and tried to beat out the flames, but they quickly spread, and soon the whole barn was afire. He tried desperately to save the livestock but most of them perished in the blaze. Grandpa's body was scorched, his beard and eyebrows singed. He said afterward that he would always be haunted by the awful sound his cows made as the fire closed in on them.

Before the fire engines could arrive, the house also caught fire. Grandpa and Grandma lost almost everything they owned. Only a few household items could be salvaged. I have in my of my cupboards at home two plates that still bear the marks of surviving the fire at my grandparents' farm.

Most vivid in my mind as a child was the picture in my imagination of Grandpa trying to beat out the quickly spreading fire and then trying to rescue his animals. Fire, I learned early in life, is a fearful thing. It can get out of control, can run wild and destroy property, even human life. Like most children, I was both afraid of fire and fascinated by it. Seeing a match being struck and bursting into flame seemed like a small miracle. And when I got a bit older and was given the chore of taking out the trash to burn, I enjoyed watching the fire as it transformed paper and cardboard into ashes. I still love to sit and stare at flames dancing on the logs in a fireplace or around the campfire.

There is something about fire that grabs our attention, whether it be a roaring conflagration consuming a building or the peaceful burning of Advent candles in a church. Fire sometimes frightens, sometimes fascinates. It invites or repels. But fire always causes a reaction. You can't ignore it.

Maybe that's why fire is an important symbol in nearly every religion in the world. There's something about its power for either good or evil that makes it a vivid representation about things beyond our control.

For the earliest members of the human family, fire was a remarkable discovery. Somehow it must have come from the sun, they thought, that remarkable fiery ball in the sky. And since nothing grows without the sun's light, they initiated rituals they hoped would guarantee fertility. Many of those rituals involved torches, bonfires, burning embers, and ashes. Sometimes they sacrificed animals in their fires. With horror we read in the Old Testament about religious rites practiced by neighbors of the Israelites, rites that called for throwing children into the fire as a sacrifice to the gods. Historians of religion tell us that fire sometimes symbolized an attempt to purify the people, to burn away the evil that threatened the village or the tribe.

There are vestiges of these old beliefs present in the Bible. You may remember the story of Abraham preparing to sacrifice his son Isaac to Yahweh, to kill the boy and then to lay the body on the altar for burning. But Yahweh intervened at the last moment. This was only a test of Abraham's faith, we are told.

I shiver when I hear some of those old stories. And as I skim through the many references to fire in the Bible, I can't help but notice that most of them have something to do with the power and wrath of God, with God's judgment. The prophet Isaiah warned:

> See, the name of the Lord comes from far away, burning with his anger, and in thick rising smoke; his lips are full of indignation, and his tongue is like a devouring fire.

Anyone who has ever been near a fire roaring out of control can understand why people of ancient time would associate fire with the anger of the god they worshiped. Fire on the rampage has an angry sound to it; it consumes everything in its path, it rages on until it burns itself out.

But what is it that could rouse Yahweh to such anger? For many of the gods in ancient times, divine wrath was unpredictable. A god's anger might blaze forth for no apparent reason. Priests had to keep bribing the gods to keep them in a good mood.

But for the people of Israel, it was a different story. The wrath of their God did not blaze forth without reason or without warning. What angered Yahweh was wrong doing, injustice, great or small. Listen to the words of the prophet Jeremiah.

Thus says the Lord:

> Execute justice in the morning, and deliver from the hand of the oppressor anyone who has been robbed, or else my wrath will go forth like fire, and burn, with no one to quench it, because of your evil doings (Isaiah 30:27).

Yahweh is a God of righteousness, Jeremiah said. If you think you can get away with cheating your neighbor and oppressing the poor, you're sadly mistaken. If you break God's law, you'd better stand back, because fire is on its way.

That kind of preaching did not win Jeremiah any awards as preacher of the year. He didn't get invited to the king's palace for afternoon tea. Let's face it, most people aren't especially fond of hearing much about God's anger. These days we mostly joke about fire and brimstone sermons. They aren't much in vogue anymore. You would be shocked to hear me cut loose with one of those old fashioned 'you'd better mend your ways or be damned to hell fire' sermons.

You won't hear a sermon like that from me because I believe that religion based on fear is a perversion of the gospel. Yet I must tell you that judgment is an essential part of our faith story. It's not the pleasant part, to be sure. It's much easier and more pleasant to emphasize stories of creation, love, and grace. But if you strip away all references to judgment, you take the fire out of the gospel. It becomes a pale and anemic thing, a sentimental, romanticized religiosity that lacks the power to change human lives.

"Our God is a consuming fire," says the writer of Hebrews, and you can bet God's judgment was what the writer had in mind. The fire of judgment is an inescapable element of our faith. Why? Not because God is a malicious deity who enjoys making people suffer. Not at all. Judgment in God's hands is a blessing, not a punishment. A severe blessing, it's true, but a blessing nonetheless.

Do you remember when you were a youngster and you did something wrong? Perhaps you pinched your baby brother or told a lie or took something that didn't belong to you. Your parents or someone who loved you acted as judge. You had to go to your room or got your fingers smacked or something else unpleasant. Looking back on it, you understand now what a blessing it was to have someone set you right in love. How much worse it would have been to have your wrongdoing ignored or condoned.

God's judgment is like that. Sometimes we feel God's judgment when a friend or colleague shows us how we are hurting others or ourselves. Sometimes we feel God's judgment when our conscience tells us we are doing wrong. Sometimes we feel God's judgment mostly as an absence or void in our lives, and we know we must do something fill that void.

Why do we need the fire of God's judgment? Because we are sometimes lazy and sometimes selfish and unkind and cynical and prejudiced and violent and foolish and all the rest. I don't know much about the process of refining iron ore to produce steel, but I know enough to realize that you don't get much of a product if you don't have fire hot enough to burn away the impurities.

Once, many centuries ago, a prophet named Malachi announced that the Lord was coming. The Lord will send a messenger to prepare the way, and then the Lord will appear. Hey, that's great news! the people thought. Let's have a party, lots to eat and drink, a parade — fireworks!

Wait, Malachi wasn't finished. He said: "But who can endure the day of his coming, and who can stand when he appears? For he is like a refiner's fire …"

When the people heard those words, they thought maybe if would be better if the Lord didn't come after all. They wanted a celebration; the prophet was talking about judgment. What do we need judgment for? They wondered. Why is the Lord getting on our case? We're the good guys. If God is looking for someone to pass judgment on, God ought to pay a visit to Egypt or Syria or Babylon. We're angels compared to them.

Then a few centuries later, one day of one year in the reign of one Caesar named Tiberius, there appeared in the wilderness of Judea a scroungy looking character named John. He preached fire and smoke, and he said the Lord is coming — soon! — and the mountains will be leveled and valleys filled up and the Lord will put things straight. Trees that aren't bearing fruit will be cut down and tossed into the fire. (Everybody knew John wasn't really talking about trees at all.) John said, baptism with water like I'm doing is one thing, but wait until he comes …fire baptism!

The people who listened to John thought it might be best for all concerned if the Lord decided to wait awhile. With all that *fire* around, they might get burned. The kind of thing they had in mind when the Lord came was some heavy number laid on their enemies, starting with scum like the Romans. But it didn't sound to them like John was talking about the Romans.

So thanks, Lord, but *no, thanks.*

The Lord came anyway — whether we are ready for it or not. Have you ever noticed how people are usually reluctant to come up close to the manger and take a long, lingering look? At best they snatch a quick glance, and usually they see only a baby. They don't stay around long enough to see the fire.

You see, before the babe in the manger can bring us joy, he must first bring us pain. We've got to see in that little child God's judgment — that there are children today born in stables, born into grinding poverty from which they will never escape and that our indifference to their pain is grievous sin. When we dare to look into the manger, we will see their loneliness, fear, and suffering, and some of it, God knows, we carry in our own hearts.

My friends, let us say "yes" to the fire. Let us accept the judgment so God may refine us, purify us, and make us strong to love justice and practice compassion. Then all the many kinds of getting ready for the Lord's coming will have a purpose. The longing in our hearts for his coming will find an answer. It will be an answer of grace, of beauty and we will see in the child's face God's love-promise. We will feel it, know it, and receive it gladly.

And the child will be Immanuel — God-with-us.

GOD IS LIKE ... A COMFORTER

2 Corinthians 1:3-7

If you were asked to name the invention that has had the greatest impact on daily life in the past century, what would you say? The electric light bulb, the automobile? You could make a strong case for either of them. I'd add another to the list: central heating.

Some of you, like me, grew up in homes that had no central heating. You may remember gathering around the kitchen stove to change clothes in the morning and going up the stairs at night to a frigid bedroom. You'd crawl between icy sheets and then pull up over you a thick, heavy, quilted blanket that you called, most appropriately, the comforter. It took a couple minutes for your body heat to warm your place in the bed, but then the comforter made its presence felt. You were warm and cozy.

Some of you may have an old patchwork comforter at your house; perhaps you have children who use it on their beds sometimes. Maybe they like to snuggle underneath its bulky warmth. But there is no way they can appreciate its merits the way I did when I was a youngster. It takes a bedroom with a temperature near the freezing mark for a comforter to truly live up to its name.

God is like a comforter. That's the title of my sermon, and it is another in our *What Is God Like?* series. We have explored together what it means to think of God as a name, as a potter, as a parent, as fire. We've considered some of the positive things that come from such symbols for God, and we've noted that while each of them is in some way appropriate, none of them is adequate to embrace all that God is.

The same is true for the notion that God is like a comforter. In fact, this symbol for God is especially tricky. We need to look at some of the positive aspects of God as comforter and then to note the negatives as well.

The place to begin, of course, is with scripture; and there are many references to choose from. Let's consider a few of the best known references to the comforting nature of God.

"The Lord is my shepherd…." begins the best loved chapter in the Bible. Halfway through Psalm 23 we find the psalmist saying to the divine shepherd: "Thy rod and thy staff they comfort me."

The prophet Isaiah painted an appealing picture of a nurturing God. In the last chapter of Isaiah, God is speaking with these words: "As a mother comforts her child, so I will comfort you …" (Isaiah 66:13).

In the book of Acts, the early church is described as "living in the fear of the Lord and in the comfort of the Holy Spirit" so that its numbers increased (Acts 9:31).

Finally, we recall the words of Jesus in that list of blessings we call the Beatitudes. "Blessed are those who mourn," said our Lord, "for they will be comforted" (Matthew 5:4).

To think of God as comforter is to expand our understanding beyond the image of a thick bed covering. There are many ways of providing comfort besides providing warmth and security. In fact, there were some drawbacks to having that heavy blanket lying on top of you. It was so heavy you could hardly move! The comfort God gives does not weigh us down; it sets us free to move, to live.

What is the definition of the verb "to comfort"? In common usage, it means (and this is the definition my dictionary gives) "to soothe in time of grief or fear, to console." The scripture references we looked at underscore that definition. Jesus spoke of God comforting those who mourn. During times of grief, of great personal loss, everyone needs comforting, needs reassurance that their friends care for them, hurt with them. Those of you who have experienced the death of a loved one or the loss of someone close to you through other kinds of separation know how comforting it is to have people reach out to you.

A mother comforting a child — that is the picture the prophet Isaiah painted of how God comforts. When do children need comfort? For a small child it's when he takes a tumble down the stairs or gets his finger pinched in a cupboard door. For an older child it may be a rough day at school when a classmate hurts her feelings. For a teenager, comfort is needed when an injustice is suffered at the hands of a teacher or a friend. Fathers can give comfort too, of course, but Isaiah chose the image of God as a mother comforting her child. Take a moment and picture it in your mind — a mother rocking her child in her arms, kissing away the tears. That's how God comforts us, said Isaiah.

Each of us has times when we need nothing so much as we need to be soothed, consoled, comforted — not just when we are children. A tough day at work, a personal disappointment, a worrisome trip to the doctor — these and many other occasions make us ache to be comforted, no matter what our age.

One way God comforts us at such times is through other people: friends, loved ones, fellow church members. God also comforts in less visible ways too; we sense deep within ourselves that God is present in our pain.

When I was twelve, my grandmother died unexpectedly. I remember the day we got the news. It was a Saturday; our family was eating the noon meal. The phone rang and my mother answered. She came back to the table and said, "Grandma Gibble passed away." No one said anything, but the radio was playing. It was tuned to a station playing religious music, and I remember very clearly the song that was being sung. The opening words to it asked a question: "Does Jesus care when my heart is pained, too deeply for mirth or song?" And then came the answer: "Oh yes, he cares. I know he cares. His heart is touched with my grief." And then something happened that froze those moments in my memory. My dad began to cry. It was a rare thing for him. The words of that song released tears of healing. God's heart touched with our grief.

God is like a comforter, but there are dangers with this understanding of God. For some people, that's all there is to God.

They want comfort, not just at times of loss or fear, but all the time. They want to be soothed and indulged constantly. Their faith never grows beyond childhood faith. They want a God who coddles them, pampers them, makes them feel good.

Some psychologists tell us that religion can become an addiction. Some people use God like a giant aspirin tablet. They want an escape from their troubles, they want to feel good. Instead of confronting their problems honestly and directly, they enlist God to make their troubles go away.

When our faith becomes little more than "what's in it for me?" it becomes childish, self-indulgent. It seeks consolation without challenge and comfort without commitment.

We must return to that word "comfort." When I looked into the origin of the word, I made a surprising discovery. The ancient root of the word "comfort" does not imply being soothed or pacified. Instead it implies strength, power, as in the words "force," "fortress," and "fortify." The original meaning of "comfort" was "to support, to give strength to."

With this meaning in mind, the scriptures cited earlier take on a different flavor. We can understand better that the divine shepherd's rod and staff could "give strength to" the psalmist. We realize that when the early church is described in Acts as living in "the comfort of the Holy Spirit, it is a reference, not to the Holy Spirit's sympathy, but to the Spirit's empowerment.

In the King James Version of John's gospel, when Jesus announced he would be leaving the disciples, he said, "If I go not away, the comforter will not come unto you" (John 16:7). More recent translations substitute "counselor" or "helper" for "comforter." But if we remember the original definition of "comfort" as "giving strength to," it makes perfect sense for Jesus to refer to the Holy Spirit as "comforter." The comforter, the Holy Spirit, will give the disciples the strength they need to carry on when Jesus is no longer with them.

In the five verses that formed this morning's scripture lesson, the apostle Paul used the word "comfort" no fewer than nine times. He said that God was "the Father of mercies and

God of all comfort." Paul asserted that God "comforts us in our affliction."

Paul was referring to the trials and persecutions that he had suffered and that the Christians in Corinth were undergoing. When you're going through that kind of trouble, you don't need something to soothe you as much as you need someone to provide you with strength to endure. And that's the kind of comfort God offers.

As members of Christ's body, we are called to comfort one another. There are times when such comfort will take the form of condolence and expressions of sympathy. But let us be careful not to forget the more dynamic definition of comfort.

We do not truly comfort people by indulging them in their childish actions or by rewarding their unhealthy behavior. If you know people who are always complaining about their boss, their spouse, or whatever, you need to listen a time or two. But after that, it becomes a disservice just to listen. You need to ask them, "What are you going to do about it?" At some point, you may even need to say, "Don't tell me about this again until you've done some positive to change the situation." That is comforting in the sense of giving strength.

You don't help your friends by doing for them what they need to do for themselves. It's a mistake to cater to their weaknesses. It's a gift to name and affirm their God-given strengths, to support them as they try their wings, to help them up and bandage their bruises if they crash, and then to insist they try again.

When I was in preaching class in seminary, I learned the old proverb that a preacher's job is to comfort the afflicted and afflict the comfortable. That's much too simplistic, of course, but it contains a measure of truth. Comforting the afflicted and afflicting the comfortable is a job not just for the preacher, but for all of us in the church.

God is like a comforter. That's true. But the comfort God has for us may make us uncomfortable in the short run. However, it isn't the short run God has in mind for us. It's the long run, the journey we call faith, the one that stretches out ahead to eternity. And for that journey, you and I need all the strength, all the comfort, God can give us.

GOD IS LIKE ... A FACE

Genesis 33:1-11; 2 Corinthians 4:5-6

God is like ...a face. What a strange idea. Of all the understandings of God we've explored thus far in this series, this is surely the most farfetched. What can it possibly mean to think of God as a face?

To answer this question we must consider the breadth and the limitation of human imagination. You and I have minds that can take us beyond the time and place where we are. We can imagine what it might have been like to live a century ago, a millennium ago. We can move, in our minds, from where we are not, to Chicago, to San Francisco, to any place we have previously been or have seen only in pictures. There seem to be no limits to our imagination.

But there are limits. We cannot imagine a world without time or space. We cannot imagine a god without human attributes. Whenever we try to describe the mystery called God, we resort to human categories. We say that God is compassionate, just, merciful. We speak of God's anger, God's faithfulness, God's love. Those are all human qualities. True, we may say that God is all-knowing, all-powerful, whereas human beings are not. But knowledge and power are things that humans experience. There is no other way to talk of God, to think of God, but in human terms.

When the people called the Hebrews attempted to describe Yahweh, their god, they emphasized Yahweh's voice. Yahweh spoke to Adam and Eve, to Noah, to Abraham and Sarah, to Moses. Yahweh spoke, yes, but Yahweh also listened.

In their psalms the people of Israel prayed:

> O Lord God of hosts, hear my prayer; give ear, O God of Jacob! Behold our shield, O God; look on the face of your anointed (Psalm 84:8-9).

Not only could God speak, God could hear, God could see. In human terms, speaking, hearing, and seeing are actions performed by the head. In most cases, when I speak or listen to or look at a person, I turn my eyes to that person's face. It was understandable, then, that the people of Israel would imagine Yahweh with a face.

They believed that Yahweh's face was too holy for mortals to look upon. As one of the ten commandments expressed it, no images were permitted to be built depicting Yahweh's body or face. And yet ... the Hebrews could not resist speaking of the face of God.

To imagine, to speak, of God's face is to imagine and speak metaphorically. In one sense, it is nonsensical to say God is like a face, just as it is nonsensical to say God is like a shepherd or like a father or like anything else. That's because any metaphor we use can only hint at the nature of the being we call God. The fathers we have known, the shepherds we've read about, the faces we have seen, are much too limited to encompass all that God is. Nevertheless, we resort to such metaphors because, without them, we cannot talk of God at all.

In the scriptures we call the Old Testament, the Hebrew word that is translated into the English word "face," also means "presence." For example, in the fourth chapter of Genesis it says that Cain, after killing his brother Abel, "went away from the presence of the Lord" (4:16). That word "presence" could also be translated "face."

In the book of Exodus, there is a fascinating episode about Moses and God. Moses had had a hard time leading the people of Israel through the wilderness. It had been a thankless job; the people were always complaining, they wanted to turn back, then they built a golden calf. Moses had had it. So Moses complained to God, and God said, "My presence will go with you, and I will give you rest." There's that word "presence" that also means "face." God was saying, "My face will go with you."

But Moses wasn't satisfied. He said to God, "Show me your glory." That's a risky thing to say to God, of course, but God agreed to it. "I will make all my goodness pass before you," God said, "but you cannot see my face; for no one shall see me and live." God told Moses to stand on a rock and said to Moses, "while my glory passes by I will put you in a cleft of the rock, and I will cover you with my hand until I have passed by; then I will take away my hand, and you shall see my back; but my face shall not be seen" (Exodus 323:23-33). It's a wonderful passage of scripture — God wanting to Moses to see the glory, but not wanting Moses to be destroyed by it. I'll let you see my back, God said, but not my face.

No one can look on God's face — that was understood. Yet in the Psalms, we find prayers for the opportunity to see God's face. Not in a literal sense, of course, but in a figurative sense.

Your face, Lord, do I seek.

Do not hide your face from me.

So exclaims the psalmist (Psalm 27:8b-9a). In another prayer, a desperate prayer, the psalmist cried:

> How long, O Lord? Will you forget me forever? How long will you hide your face from me?" (Psalm 13:1).We find in the scriptures what appears to be contradictory feelings about seeing the face of God. The thought of looking on God's face is a terrifying prospect said the Old Testament writers; yet if God's face is turned away from us, we fall into despair.

When we come to the New Testament, we encounter the faith of people who believed that in Jesus of Nazareth, God was fully present. The apostle Paul wrote that the glory of God is visible "in the face of Jesus Christ" (2 Corinthians 4:6c).

The face of Jesus Christ. Doesn't it strike you as odd that there is not a description of what Jesus looked like anywhere in the New Testament? Was he short or tall? Was he thin or muscular? Was his face handsome or homely? We just don't know. Apparently, what Jesus looked like wasn't all that important.

The only times the face of Jesus is mentioned are, first, on that mysterious occasion called the Transfiguration, where his face was described as shining like the sun; second, in Luke where we are told he "set his face to go to Jerusalem"; and finally at his trial where his tormentors spit in his face and struck his face.

And yet, despite this surprising scarcity of references to the face of Jesus, Paul insisted on saying that in the face of Jesus Christ we see the glory of God.

How do you picture the face of Jesus? For many people in this country, that face is the one depicted by the painter Sallman, in which Jesus is a handsome, blue-eyed Anglo-Saxon. In other cultures, artists show a Jesus with Asian features or African features. That is as it should be. Jesus, in real life, probably looked like an average Semitic Jew of his time. But the Jesus Christ of faith had a face accessible to people of every race and culture. In his face, we catch a glimpse of the face of God.

Back when I first started watching television, there was a program that I tried never to miss. Every week there was a new story, and every week the story took viewers to a strange world, a world where the unusual was commonplace, where the bizarre was normal, where the improbable seemed probable or least possible.

The name of the program was "The Twilight Zone." A haunting musical theme introduced the distinctive voice of the host, Rod Serling, who welcomed viewers to a "world of enchantment," to a dimension of sight, a dimension of sound, a land of shadow and substance.

In one especially memorable episode, the characters, whose faces remained shadowed, are having an animated discussion about a strange-looking creature that had come from an unknown place. The head of this creature was kept covered because it is said to be so hideously ugly that seeing it would cause panic among the citizenry. A long discussion followed about what to do with this ugly creature. It was decided at last that, to satisfy the curiosity of everyone, the creature's face would be unveiled. The camera moved in as the covering was slowly lifted and the face was revealed. It was the face of a beautiful woman. Only then did the camera shift to the faces of the people who stood murmuring about how ugly this creature was. At last we can see that their faces were, by human standards, revoltingly distorted, unspeakably ugly. They were people of another planet, perhaps; another world.

Beauty is in the eye of the beholder, indeed. So is ugliness.

There are many faces in our world. The English writer Thomas Browne once said, "It is the common wonder of all [people], how among so many millions of faces, there should be none alike." It is a wonder, this limitless variety in the faces of the human family. Yes, despite this wondrous variety, there is a sense in which every face carries within it a reflection of the face of its creator. Each of us, after all, is made "in the image of God."

In adolescence most of us go through a stage when we despair of our faces. They are too thin, too pimply, too plain, too this, or too that. I remember learning a funny song at camp that dealt with this very theme. Sung to the tune of "Blest Be the Tie That Binds," the words went like this:

> I know how ugly I are.
> My face, it ain't no shining star.
> But I don't mind it because I'm behind it.
> The fellow in front gets the jar. (in the public domain)

To some extent at least, we are all aware that our faces ain't no shining stars. Nevertheless, there is in my face, in your face, in every face ever created, the faintest glimmer of God's face.

Jacob was going to meet his brother Esau. It had been many years since they last saw each other. Jacob had run away because his brother threatened to kill him for stealing his birthright. Now they were meeting again and Jacob was frightened. Suppose his brother still wanted to kill him. Suppose Esau's face was still contorted by the anger of that past injustice. Jacob looked up ahead and saw Esau coming toward him. Jacob bowed low to the ground to show his humility. Esau ran up to him, embraced him, and kissed him. They wept in each other's arms. And Jacob sais to his brother, "Seeing your face is like seeing the face of God."

It's certainly true that with some faces it is easier to see a glimpse of God's face than with others. Sometimes, in fact, it takes a great deal of imagination to do that. Yet we remember our Lord telling his followers that when they reached out to those in need, they were reaching out to him. In the same way, when we look into the faces of those around us, we may see there the tracings of his face. And, said Jesus, "Whoever has seen me has seen the Father" (1 John 14:9b).

It helps me to believe, to trust, that God looks at every human face the way a loving mother or father looks at the face of their sleeping child — and sometimes smiles, sometimes weeps, at the beauty of that face.

All this may well be in preparation for a time, beyond time, when, as Paul put it, we will know, not in part, but fully; we will know as we are known. Now we see in a mirror dimly, but then we will see face to face (1 Corinthians 13:12).

Face to face. It's a frightening thought. It's a blessed thought. No matter how average or unusual, how beautiful or homely, how marked by age or trouble are your faces and mine, they are all loved, cherished, by the holy one who made them and us.

The old gospel chorus put it this way:

When by his grace I shall look on his face,
That will be glory, be glory for me.
A glory indeed, a nearly unimaginable glory.
(in the public domain)

GOD IS LIKE ... A FRIEND

2 Corinthians 5:16-20

It's time for class to begin. You troop in with the rest of your classmates, you get out your notebook and pencil, and you look up front where your teacher stands ready to get started. "All right, class," she says, "let's review. What have we learned so far about Benjamin Franklin?"

Remember those days? Some of us here this morning are still students, so this scenario is all too familiar. For most of us, though, being asked to review what we've learned is something that doesn't happen much anymore. But this morning, that's how I want to begin my sermon. What are the metaphors we've used to describe God?

The answers? God is like a name, a potter, a parent, fire, a comforter, a face.

As I reviewed this list myself, I noticed something I hadn't noticed before. In nearly all of those words for God, there is a movement between nearness and farness. Theologians use fancier words; they talk about the tension between immanence and transcendence. That is, on the one hand, we can describe God as being very close to us, even within us; on the other hand, God can be described as being apart from us, above us, beyond us.

Our relationship with God keeps moving back and forth between intimacy and distance. For example, if you think of God as fire, you may remember how Moses saw a burning bush and how awestruck Moses was by the wondrous power of God. But you may also remember how the disciples met their risen Lord on the road to Emmaus and felt their hearts burn within them. To think of God as being like fire, then, may remind us of the "otherness" of God or, conversely, it may remind us of how the Spirit of God may warm us, energize us within.

Let me summarize: any worthwhile symbol or metaphor for God will contain the possibility of both immanence and transcendence, nearness and farness, intimacy and distance.

Having said that, I've set myself up to have trouble with the image for God we're going to explore this morning. When we say that God is like a friend, it appears that we've put all our eggs into the nearness basket, the imminence basket. A friend, by definition, is someone with whom you have a close, personal, intimate relationship.

Think for a moment about one of those images of God we've previously considered — God as a parent. The parent image for God does imply intimacy; few things are more intimate than the parent-child relationship. But there is distance in that relationship too. Sometimes, when we are children, our parents stand beyond us, even against us, when they are, as we say, "laying down the law." It's not really a relationship between equals.

But friendship implies that two people are pretty much on the same level, that the usual distinctions of old-young, rich-poor, smart-dumb, male-female don't apply or don't matter. That's a little hard to conjure up when it comes to a relationship with God.

It's one thing to think about the mercy of God or the judgment of God. You take off your shoes and stand as you would before a smoking mountain or a raging ocean. But the friendship of God? That would seem to be a whole different ball game.

Yet there are places in the Bible where the friendship of God is specifically mentioned. In the book of Exodus, these words are recorded: "the Lord used to speak to Moses face to face, as one speaks to a friend" (Exodus 33:11). And in several books in the Bible, it is said that Abraham was "the friend of God" (Isaiah 41:8, 2 Chronicles 20:7, James 2:23).

Exactly what the biblical writers meant by that, of course, is hard to say. What picture do you get in your mind when you hear Moses and Abraham described as God's friends?

That's an attractive picture, I think, but it is, after all, only that — a picture. You are not Moses, nor Abraham. Neither am I. What chance is there for God to be your friend, my friend?

To get help on this question, we turn to our scripture readings for the morning. The Good News translation, sometimes called Today's English Version, offers a helpful rendering of an often-quoted passage, often-quoted because it summarizes so well one of the central beliefs of Christianity — the idea that God has acted to remove whatever keeps people separated from God. Here again are a few verses from the fifth chapter of Second Corinthians, this time from the Good News translation.

> When anyone is joined to Christ, he [or she] is a new being; the old is gone, the new has come. All this is from God, who through Christ changed us from enemies into his friends and gave us the task of making others his friends also.

That's quite a statement, isn't it? If sin is what separates us from God, in Christ we see God acting to forgive our sin. Instead of a broken relationship with God, we are given a restored relationship. No longer is God our judge, our enemy; God is now our friend.

You may be familiar with a gospel hymn that presents a poetic picture of an intimate relationship with God. It contains these words: "My God and I go in the field together; we walk and talk as good friends should and do. We clasp our hands, our voices ring with laughter...." Lovely words, to be sure, but they are, after all, poetry. You and I cannot see or touch God, after all, not as we can see and touch a man or woman, a boy or girl, who is our friend. That's why, for many Christians, the person of Jesus becomes the human link between themselves and God. In the fourth Gospel, the one called John, we hear Jesus speaking to his disciples.

> This is my commandment, that you love one another as I have loved you. No one has greater love than this, to lay down one's life for one's friends. You are my friends if

you do what I command you. I do not call you servants any longer, because the servant does not know what the master is doing; but I have called you friends .... (John 15:12-5).

"What a friend we have in Jesus" run the words of a beloved old hymn, and surely what has made it beloved is the imagery of having Jesus as an intimate companion, someone you can pour out all your troubles to, someone you can count on to be there support and encouragement.

The friendship of Jesus teaches us to be friends to others. In the human face of Jesus, we see the friendship of God made plain. We are given the promise of being the friends of Jesus if we will do what he commands. And the commandment is simple, yet daunting — to love one another. To be his friend, we have to be friends with each other. We may even be called upon to lay down our lives for each other, as he did for us. This is not fair weather friendship we're talking about, folks. This is friendship by the divine standard, and a high standard it is.

Friendship on the human level is something we all want and all too rarely find. I'm speaking now about friendship that lasts, that goes through the good times and the bad times, that deepens and grows stronger.

The old proverb says that the only way to have a friend is to be one. It's true. Real friendship involves hard work. It means keeping open the lines of communication, it means taking the time and energy needed to keep the friendship alive and growing. It means being willing to be both honest and loving in equal measure. It will sometimes require personal sacrifice for the good of the other person.

Friendship demands something of us, but what a gift it is. As someone has said, your friends are not your friends for any particular reason. Friends are people you make part of your life just because you want to. Your job, your family, your political preferences, your religious convictions, your personal successes or failures aren't really what matter. What matters is a relationship that has been tested by time and circumstance, both the easy and good as well as the difficult. Friendship is based on mutual trust.

It's much the same with friendship with God. Implanted within us is a longing to have this friendship too. I said at the outset that thinking of God as friend may imply only closeness, not distance. But in all human friendships that last for a period of time, there are times when we do not feel close to our friends. They may be busy with other matters, they may move to another location, they may distance themselves for any number of reasons. Human friendships often wax and wane, like the phases of the moon.

In our friendship with God, we will also have times of feeling apart, rather than close to God. Like any human friendship, friendship with God demands something of us. Specifically, it demands an intentional effort to cultivate that friendship. Prayer and meditation are two ways to accomplish that. One person I know of says that when he was going through an especially lonely time in his life, he began his prayers with the words "Infinite Friend."

About the time I graduated from college, I attended a weekend for young adults at our church camp. The leader for the weekend was a young pastor who prayed in a way that left an impression on me. Most of the prayers I had heard in worship and other places seemed like they were being lifted up to the sky to the throne of a distant, remote deity. But the prayers I heard on this weekend were different. Our leader prayed in conversational style. It was almost as if he were talking to …well, a friend. The prayers were honest, straightforward. They included simple statements about what the person praying them was feeling. There were no long words or convoluted sentences. There was no "churchy" vocabulary and, for the first time, I think, I realized that prayer was something I could do without pretending to be somebody I wasn't.

Maybe that's really what God as friend is all about. God says to us: with me you can be yourself. You don't have to put up a front. You don't have to wear a disguise. I accept you as you are.

God says, *your life has already has its ups and downs and you can bet there will be more of the same. Beautiful and terrible things will happen. Don't be afraid. I promise to go with you through the whole business. I love you. Nothing can ever separate us.*

Friendship with God — does it sound too good to be true? It's not; it's offered to you free of charge. But there is a catch. In order to have it, you've got to reach out and take it.

So …take it. What are you waiting for?

GOD IS LIKE ... A LAMB

Exodus 12:3-8; Luke 22:7-20

What's the first song you ever learned? There are some perennial children's favorites, such as "Twinkle, Twinkle, Little Star" and in Sunday school, "Jesus Loves Me, This I Know." But the odds are pretty good that for some of you here this morning, one of the first songs or maybe even the very first song you learned was "Mary Had a Little Lamb."

What an interesting lamb it was, not because its fleece was white as snow, but because of what it did ...it followed Mary everywhere. One day it even followed her ...where? Yes, to school. The song tells us that such behavior in a lamb was against the rule. I should think so. I mean, children have a hard enough time getting down to their studies without a lamb frolicking about in the classroom. The song tells us that "it made the children laugh and play to see a lamb at school."

Most printed versions of the song I've seen end with this upbeat verse about the children laughing and playing. But I remember another final verse, one that I learned from hearing my mother sing it. "... so the teacher turned it out, turned it out, turned it out. ... so the teacher turned it out, which made the children cry." I'm sure my mother's intention was not to teach me that life is tragic, but in that version I learned as a child, it was clear that deviant behavior by both lambs and owners of lambs would result in tearful consequences. Children laughing and playing might be all well and good on holidays, but school time was work time. Teachers were there to insure that lambs, even lambs as loyal as Mary's, did not interfere with the serious business of learning.

By the way, sometimes my research for sermons turns up some interesting, though not especially relevant, information. I can't resist passing on a bit of trivia I uncovered. "Mary Had a Little Lamb" was written by one Sarah Josepha Hale of

Boston, who was one of the best-known magazine editors of the nineteenth century. It was she who reportedly persuaded Abraham Lincoln to make Thanksgiving a national holiday. She was a prolific writer and a celebrity in her own day. Ironically, more than a hundred years after her death, the only thing Sarah Josepha Hale wrote that people still remember is her children's verse about Mary and her lamb.

By now it should be obvious to you that all this business about a lamb is leading up to something preachy. This is a sermon, after all, not a lecture on the history of nursery rhymes. " GOD IS LIKE …a Lamb" is the title of today's sermon, so it's time to explore the meaning of this rather unusual metaphor.

We begin by recalling the story of the Passover. On the eve of their departure from slavery in Egypt, the Israelites were told by Moses to take a lamb without blemish and to slaughter it for a last meal. Some blood of the slain lamb was to be sprinkled on the doorpost so the angel of death would "pass over" their house and visit only the houses of the Egyptians. So was instituted the feast of Passover, a ritual still observed, thousands of years later, by people of the Jewish faith.

Why was a lamb chosen for this ritual? We don't know. Was it because, even in ancient times, the lamb symbolized innocence? Perhaps. The sacrifice of young animals, especially lambs, goes way back in human history. Slaughtering a lamb was thought by many ancient peoples to be a means of appeasing the gods. In ancient Israel, sacrifice of animals was part of the ritual for removing sin and guilt.

In our New Testament reading from Luke, we find Jesus sending two of his disciples to make preparations for the Passover supper. Luke specifically mentions the animal that is central to this meal, the Passover lamb. Finally all preparations were completed and Jesus took his place at the table with his companions. He said to them: "I have eagerly desired to eat this Passover meal with you before I suffer." Then he took bread and said, "This is my body, which is given for you. Do this in remembrance of me." Then he took wine and said, "This cup that is poured out for you is the new covenant in my blood."

I'm sure you recognize in those words what we use as part of our celebrations of Holy Communion. What you may not recognize is the connection Jesus makes between the blood of the Passover lamb and his own blood. When the early Christians looked back on all that Jesus said and did while he was with them, they saw God's hand at work in the life, death, and resurrection of Jesus.

Why, they said, Jesus was himself the Passover lamb. Just as the blood of the first Passover lamb made possible the liberation of the children of Israel, so the blood of Jesus the crucified, Passover lamb sets us free, free from sin and guilt, free to be a new Israel, a new creation.

They remembered the words from Isaiah who spoke about a suffering servant who "was wounded for our transgressions, crushed for our iniquities," who "was oppressed …and afflicted, yet he did not open his mouth; like a lamb that is led to the slaughter …" (Isaiah 53:5,7, see also Acts 8:32).

For the first Christians, there could be no doubt that Isaiah was looking ahead to the ordeal that Jesus would endure in his trial and crucifixion. Paul wrote in 1 Corinthians that Christ was our Passover lamb sacrificed for us (1 Corinthians 5:7). In Peter's first letter, he wrote to his Christian friends to remind them that they have been ransomed "with the precious blood of Christ, like that of a lamb without defect or blemish" (1 Peter 1:19). When the fourth gospel came to be written, the writer included a scene which found John the Baptist seeing Jesus for the first time. John pointed to Jesus and said, "Here is the Lamb of God who takes away the sin of the world!" (John 1:29).

Convinced that Jesus was God's own beloved Son, the Christian believers made very clear their belief that Jesus had been sent by God to fulfill God's purposes. One of those purposes was to become the lamb led to sacrifice in order to free the human family from sin and guilt. What an audacious claim the believers were making — that God, as we see God in Christ, is like a lamb.

God like a lamb? At first thought, it's an outrageous idea. Lambs are frail, helpless creatures, totally dependent on their mother for nourishment and guidance. Lambs are weak, easy victims of predators. The English poet, William Blake, summarized beautifully how we usually think of lambs. He imagined a child speaking to a lamb frolicking in the meadow.

> Little Lamb, who made thee?
> Dost thou know who made thee?
> Gave thee life, and bid thee feed,
> By the stream and o'er the mead;
> Gave thee clothing of delight,
> Softest clothing, woolly, bright;
> Gave thee such a tender voice,
> Making all the vales rejoice?
> Little Lamb, who made thee?
> Dost thou know who made thee?

And then Blake answered the question he asked of the lamb and made a connection between the lamb in the pasture and the one whom Christians call the Lamb of God.

> Little lamb, I'll tell thee,
> Little lamb, I'll tell thee:
> He is called by thy name,
> For He calls himself a Lamb,
> He is meek, and He is mild;
> He became a little child.
> I a child, and thou a lamb,
> We are called by His name.
> Little Lamb, God bless thee!
> Little Lamb, God bless thee! (in the public domain)

Lambs are meek, mild, innocent animals. Isn't it preposterous to think of God, the Almighty Creator of the universe, as being lamb-like? Frankly, yes. But in the last book of the Bible, the book called Revelation, we come to something even more outrageous (see Revelation 5).

The scene is heaven where the angels are assembled before God seated on a throne. In God's hand is a scroll that contains the fixed purposes of God for the future. And the cry goes up: "Who is worthy to open the scroll?" At first, no one in heaven is found, and John, who was writing this account, tells us he wept because no one was worthy to reveal God's purposes. But an angel came to John and said, "See, the lion of the tribe of Judah, the root of David, has conquered, so that he can open the scroll."

This was great news, but as John looked for the lion of Judah, he was astonished to see instead a lamb, "Standing as if it had been slaughtered." And the heavenly host burst into an anthem:

> Worthy is the Lamb that was slaughtered
> to receive power and wealth and wisdom and might
> and honor and glory and blessing!
> And then the Lamb opens the scroll to reveal
> God's purposes.

What in the world did this fantastic vision mean? Obviously, it has many layers of meaning, but one thing is clear. The lamb isn't just a lamb, after all, but a fierce lion. Both the lamb and the lion are symbols for Christ. To say it another way, God is like a lamb … and God is also like a lion.

We have to go back to Genesis to find the first reference to the lion of Judah (Genesis 49:9). Later on, David, the mighty warrior, who came from the tribe of Judah, became known as the lion of Judah. For centuries, the people of Israel waited for a descendant of David, a messiah, a savior, to come as the new lion of Judah. Why a lion? Because that animal symbolizes raw strength, brutal power.

This lion, this fierce, powerful creature, turned out, in the book of Revelation, to be, of all things, a lamb. What does the Bible mean by mixing these metaphors for Christ, for God? How can the lion be the lamb? How can the lamb be a lion?

If we think in terms of what the cross means, we see how God's willing sacrifice, the death of Jesus, turned out to be God's greatest triumph. Oddly enough, the lamb's very defenselessness is its lion-like strength.

That is, God's method of showing power was revealed in what appeared to be weakness. Jesus, Lord of lords, came into the world as a helpless infant born to a peasant woman. The Messiah, of the lineage of King David, the warrior lion, rode into Jerusalem, not on the back of a fiery warhorse, but astride a donkey, the humble work animal of the common folk. Christ, who is King of kings, was inaugurated with a crown of thorns and was enthroned on a gallows on which a cynical Roman governor hung a sign that read: "Jesus of Nazareth, King of the Jews." Pilate meant it as gallows humor — as a derisive joke. But the joke, it turned out, was on Pilate and ultimately on all those who thought they and their kind were in charge.

In the end, the victory belongs to God. The apostle Paul said it best. God's power "is made perfect in weakness," wrote Paul (2 Corinthians 12:9). That is the mystery that turns the common perception of things on their ears. It is the mystery of God's all-conquering, lion-like love revealed in the Lamb of God who takes away the sin of the world.

We stake our lives on this mystery, we followers of the lamb. Though it is sometimes hard, we pledge not to return evil for evil, but to return good for evil. We reject the motto that might makes right and instead, with God's help, choose to live by the law of love, doing to others as we would have them do to us. Though we are sometimes fearful, we dare to believe God's word that perfect love casts out fear.

God is like a lamb and God is like a lion as well, two sides of the coin we call God's love. That love is the key to the mystery.

Love is also the key to understanding that song we learned as children. It turns out that my mother was wrong about the last verse of the song. It has taken me all these years to find out what the last verse written by Sarah Josepha Hale really was. I know, because I looked it up. Here it is.

"What makes the lamb love Mary so?"
The eager children cry.
"Why, Mary loves the lamb, you know,"
The teacher did reply.

She was a wise teacher to understand that love is what makes it happen. It was another Mary, wasn't it, who loved another lamb she held in her arms and named Jesus? He was the Lamb of God, the lamb who was the lion, who loves us all with God's holy love, a fierce, enduring love; love that will never let us go.

GOD IS LIKE ...

Isaiah 40:18-31; John 1:1-14

With some things, once you get started, it's hard to stop. Things like eating salted peanuts and reading a good murder mystery and doing a challenging crossword puzzle. Or, in my own case, preaching sermons in a series entitled "God is like . . ."

In that first sermon of the series I said:

> My purpose is simply to help all of us appreciate and understand more about God and to discover appropriate responses to this Holy One. I hope our exploration will provide both comfort and challenge. And I expect some surprises along the way, because what I keep discovering is that the universe we live in and the God who creates it are more complex and more wonderful than we can imagine.

Looking back on that statement of purpose in preparation for this sermon, I discovered that, whatever benefit our exploration may have had for members of this congregation (and only you can be the judges of that), my own faith experience has been deepened and broadened. There were indeed some surprises along the way, images and metaphors for God that took on new meaning for me. I needed and received reminders of how much more there is to this mystery we call God than we suppose. You and I have a natural inclination to reduce God to manageable size, to confine God within safe and familiar categories. We make the sad mistake of preferring God on our terms, rather than on God's terms. The Holy One is far greater and wilder and more wonderful than we dare to imagine.

As I said, once I got started on this journey called "God is like. . .," it was hard to stop. This series has gone on longer than I originally planned. About the time I thought a particular installment would be the last, I would stumble upon something in the scripture or elsewhere that nudged me onward. But, as my dad used to tell me, all good things must come to an end. After all, one can run a good thing into the ground.

So this reflection is the formal ending to the series, a kind of wrap up to our journey. But maybe, by the grace of God, these explorations can be a gestation for the faith that is yet to be born. Instead of an ending, we may think of it as a new beginning, a challenge for all of us to keep growing in our understanding of what and who God is, of what and who God calls us to become.

As I contemplated an appropriate way to conclude this series, I decided to draw on some of the readings that had been especially helpful to me along the way, writers both ancient and modern who pushed me to expand my understanding of God. I want to share some of those resources with you.

The obvious place to begin is with the Bible. As I searched for an appropriate text, I came again to that wonderful chapter 40 in the book of Isaiah. The opening verses are very familiar because we read them during the Advent season: "Comfort ye, comfort ye my people, saith your God."

The second half of the chapter is not as well known, but how relevant it is to our theme. Verse 18 begins with a question: "To whom then will you liken God, or what likeness compare with him?" This question is addressed to people who have been guilty of breaking the second commandment. That commandment says: "You shall not make for yourself an idol," or "graven image," as the King James Version puts it.

Have you ever wondered why that is one of the commandments? It doesn't seem especially relevant to us, because we are not tempted to construct images of wood or stone and bow down to them. But for people in ancient Israel, idols were a temptation. They found it frustrating to worship a god they could not see or hear or touch. How much more comforting to see what you are praying to. The danger of such images, of course, is that the worshipers reduce their god to manageable, controllable size. And one thing we simply cannot do is control God.

No less than the people of ancient Israel, you and I are tempted to keep God confined to convenient, controllable categories. God can be this, we think, but God couldn't possibly be that. God is masculine, a father, a "he." God couldn't possibly be also feminine, a mother, a "she." Oh no? Says who? "To whom then will you compare me," asks God in Isaiah. "Who is my equal?" says the Holy One. That is a very good question. Let us not suppose any image, any metaphor of God is adequate. God is constantly pushing beyond any understanding we have of God.

And yet we must try to understand what we can. We are created with the deep need to reach beyond ourselves to the Infinite, to be in relationship with the one who called us into being.

"God is infinitely more." Maybe that phrase sums up the whole business. Yes, our language is inadequate, but you and I are creatures of language. We do most of our thinking with words. And so we keep searching for ways to express the inexpressible, to understand the un understandable.

From time to time I have attempted to use varying images for God in my prayer life. As noted earlier, Jesus frequently addressed God as Father. In what has come to be called the Lord's Prayer, the opening words employ that image. . . "Our Father who art in heaven . . ." Many prayers prayed in public settings begin with a brief form of address such as "Gracious God," "Holy One," "Loving Father" or "Loving Mother."

What follows are some of my ways I've used images of God to begin prayers.

> O Lover of all things small and great
> towering oak and modest dandelion
> tiny mole and massive humpback whale
> gentle breeze and roaring thundercloud
>
> Grace us with awakened eyes and hearts open
> to humility and wonder
> O Bread of Life, Daily Provider,
> remind us that your gift of energy

and sustenance is not for us alone
but manna to be taken and shared
with all whose hunger calls us to respond.
Empower us to feed a hungry world.

O Holy Wind that sweeps unseen across
the sprawling landscape of our lives,
blow away the fences we erect
to preserve and perpetuate our
lengthy list of selfish needs and wants.
Whisk them out of sight, out of mind.

O Steadfast Rock, O Ground of all that is,
remind us that, as seasons come and go,
as our lives progress from youth to
elderhood, your undiminished love
remains firm, steadfast, unshaken.
You are the Truth of faith's firm foundation.

O Healer of all brokenness, all ills
of body, mind and heart. Your
love and grace penetrate our pain,
tenderly invites us to see
the suffering of others, to extend
a hand of kindness and compassion.

Names, images, metaphors for God. Some of them may be helpful for you, some of them not, but all of them inadequate to express all that God is. So then, is God completely hidden from us? Are we, as Isaiah puts it, mere grasshoppers, so far removed from God's infinite majesty that we are doomed to grasp for, but never to reach God?

The answer given by our faith tradition is that, yes, our grasping for God is in vain. Our human limitations are simply too great. But that is not the end of the matter. Our faith also testifies that God, in an astounding act of boldness and grace, has reached out to us.

How does God reach out to us? In countless ways... in the wonders of the natural world; in the gift of each new day's dawning; in the eyes, the arms, the presence of people who care for us.

God in human form? Yes. That is our faith, a faith testified to by those who centuries ago saw in a man from Nazareth God revealed. In Jesus, the inconceivable was conceived. That is what the Gospel of John proclaims in its audacious prologue:

> And the Word became flesh and lived among us, and we have seen his glory, the glory as of a father's only son, full of grace and truth. (John 1:14)

This is the heart of our faith, the mark that distinguishes Christianity from other religions, each religion striving to name the unnameable, to apprehend, if only in a partial way the mystery we call God. Christianity says that God was present in Jesus the Christ, that if we want to have even a glimpse of what God is like, we can do no better than to look at Jesus, look at him with the eyes of faith, look at him with hearts open to him.

Well then, what does Jesus reveal to us about God? Many things that God cares for us, that God wants us to fulfill God's plan for creation of well being for all creatures, that God hates injustice and oppression, that God will risk anything and everything for the world God loves.

Love. That's who God is; that's what God is. "God is love," said the writer of the book we call 1 John. God is love.

God is love. So easy to say, yet how difficult to understand all that it means. How can we possibly understand it all; we are mere human beings? Fortunately for us, we don't need to understand it all. We don't need to be brilliant theologians. In fact, a childlike faith is best. That's what Jesus said one time as he put his arms around the children and drew them to him.

Near the end of Karl Barth's life, the brilliant German theologian came to this country for a speaking tour. After one of his lectures, he took questions from the audience. One question was a very unusual one. "Dr. Barth," asked the questioner, "you've written volumes of theology; you've spent your whole lifetime in the quest to understand God. If you could summarize that quest in one summary sentence, what would it be?" The great man paused for a moment, and then said:

"I'd summarize it all with these words 'Jesus loves me, this I know, for the Bible tells me so.'"

Maybe that's what it all comes down to, this search to discover what God is like. It begins and ends with the faith of a child, that Jesus loves us, that God loves us.

Why? Because God — is — love.